Thanks Jo[...]

With warmest regards, Ellyn maybe

The C[...]
of Amnesia

Ellyn Maybe

©1998 Ellyn Maybe

ISBN: 1-880985-58-6

Edited by: EXENE CERVENKOVA
Cover artwork and photographs: VIGGO MORTENSEN
Design: ENDLESS ∞

2.13.61
P.O. BOX 1910 · LOS ANGELES ·
CALIFORNIA · 90078 · USA

2.13.61 INFO HOTLINE #: (213)969-8043
www.two1361.com

ACKNOWLEDGMENTS

Thanks and appreciation to Exene Cervenkova, Viggo Mortensen,
Henry Rollins, 2.13.61's wonderful staff, Jeff McDaniel, Ron Maxson,
my mom, my grandma Anne and the benevolence of the poetry community.

CONTENTS

DO YOU FEAR ME 8

I HAVE NEVER FALLEN IN LOVE WITH ANYONE
     WHO FELT COMFORTABLE IN AMERICA 9

A DAY IN THE LIFE OF A WORKING POOR XYLOPHONE MAKER 12

I GO A LITTLE CRAZY 17

EYELID DEEP 18

WANT TO BE A STRIPPER 22

HOW I BECAME A RECORD COLLECTOR 27

THE DYSFUNCTIONAL SECULAR SERENITY PRAYER 33

HE KISSES GIRLS JUST CAUSE THEY'RE BLOND 40

I HAD THE BEST YOGURT OF MY LIFE IN BERKELEY 41

SCIENCE POEM 43

FIDO 48

CHROMAKEY CHORDS 57

I'M NOT HUNGRY LIKE THAT 65

AN ELLYN MAYBE POEM 70

NOT YET 75

BALL & CHAIN RECORD STORE 80

EARRINGS OF THE TRAIL OF TEARS 89

UMBILICAL CORD 100

ALL THIS 'CAUSE YOU'VE DOUBTED
     THAT YOU HAVE YOUR OWN 102

I HAVE FALLEN 3 TIMES 105

YOM KIPPUR BLUES 111

AN OPEN LETTER TO JOSEPH CAMPBELL 116

MY MIND IS A RADIO 121

THE COWARDICE OF AMNESIA 126

WHO'S GONNA TALK ABOUT THE SUNFLOWERS NOW 130

The
Cowardice
of
Amnesia

DO YOU FEAR ME

Do you fear me cause I wear
    a purple friendship bracelet?
Do you fear having me as a friend?
Are you afraid to introduce me
    to your grandparents?
The only perfect thing about me
    is my perfect lack of confidence.
Does that freak you out?
I'm fat.
How does that sit with you?
I wear political pins.
Does that bother you?
I'm a bookworm.
Does that depress you?
Are you terrified
    cause I've been bas mitzvahed?
Are you scared
    cause I think spiders are sacred?
I'm left handed. oooooooooooo No comment.
Do you worry about me cause I'm a virgin?
Cause I'm loud and sometimes embarrassing,
    are you wary of spending time with me?
I know where the feminist bookstores are
    in a whole bunch of states.
Does that make you tremble?
People think I'm younger
    and older than I am.
Does that reflect badly on you somehow?
I don't always comb my hair.
Can you hear it coming?
Is it my ugliness or beauty that
    frightens you the most?
Are you afraid of me cause I'm human?

I HAVE NEVER FALLEN IN LOVE WITH ANYONE WHO FELT COMFORTABLE IN AMERICA

I have never fallen in love
    with anyone who felt
    comfortable in America

people who wear the 60's
    on their eyebrows like a birthmark

who wear turn of the century Russia
    like a boat with a hull made of flame

people who wear Montreal
    like an almanac
    that is a forbidden book
    floating on their adam's apple

people who wear a T.V.
    under their arms
    like a deodorant
    trying to decide
    where the antenna belongs

people who can recite 80 poems
    but can't remember
    their driver's license
    have my respect

people who can sing 100 bottles
    of sandpaintings on the wall
    backwards
    in the time it takes
    to pour the shotglass
    that pulls its trigger slowly

people who talk to dogs
    and trees
    and are afraid
    to ask the time
    and yet somehow know
    are beloved

people who wear anthems they make
    with paisley and parsley
    and mesh together a bell
    that rings through the soundproof sky
    the government is trying to sanction

people whose fingers tell stories
    of peace and love and thunderclouds
    overcome by a dish of lightning
    with a side of stars

people who don't listen
    at the most popular
    time of day
    to the most popular
    radio station
    because they'd rather be wishing

people who have cars
    so full of bumperstickers
    the engine is only incidental

the people
    who miss card catalogs

the people who miss
    cream rising to the top
the people who yearn for deja-vu

the people who love Leonard Cohen's voice
Leonard Cohen

these are the ones I sing to
    in my overbitten sleep.

A DAY IN THE LIFE OF A
WORKING POOR XYLOPHONE MAKER

the psychedelic alarm clock that knows
    all of the songs by the byrds,
    the monkees, and various barnyard animals
    is broken so I wake up when I wake up
    and try to call time to find out
    what it is, man.

but the collection agency took my phone away
    so I put on some bellbottoms
    and trust the sun like a compass
    and try to estimate the time.
L.A. is smog urchin of the science fiction
    nightmares so my eyes begin to sweat
    like bruce springsteen's forehead
    in a bandana after a concert in wyoming.

I still don't know what time it is
    but I remember my upstairs neighbor
    has a grandfather clock so I walk upstairs
    and realize she's run off
    with my boyfriend, tire
    an automobile mechanic who only fixes
    deadhead vans.

they left a hologram for the slum landlord
I read it as best as I could with the help
    of a tiny tim strobe light
"dear slum landlord who charged a buck extra
    for rent every time we played *truckin'*
    who drew a salvador dali moustache
    on the poster of janis joplin

we're leaving this land to start
a new life defending tubas
from the threat of harmonicas."
tire used to think the feminine nombre
of el salvador was la salvador
and that they were separate countries
but agreed on *i* before *e* except after *c*.

ciao there are edible tambourines in the oven
meanwhile the oven was involved
in a court case charging brillo pads
with unnecessary cruelty.

so 1984
I went hungry and went to work at
vegetarian records and benevolent videos.
my job is at a record store that
ironically doesn't sell records.
we sell software, hard contact lenses,
guitars that gently weep,
hysterical mandolins, drums that chant,
day-glo patio furniture, compact discs
and there's a 12 inch singles dating club
for classical and rock fans who like bach
and bachman turner overdrive and know the
difference between g sharp enough to
cut glass and g dull.

my record store has only one employee
me
it has 85 bosses
there's a boss for a-l jazz / m-z punk
a boss for the tofu licorice aisle

a boss for customer bitching
a boss for my bitching
a boss for time clock grievances
a boss for sex harassments
a boss for posters of 70's disco icons
     turned talk show hosts.
a great deal of worker-employer tension
     is created by the dress code congress
on monday I wear scottish kilts
on tuesday I wear a see through blouse
     with a polka-dot bra that I burn
     just before my shift
wednesday I wear platform heels
     and dress up like a subway
thursday I wear maps in my hair
     and guitar picks in my teeth
friday I dress in a miniskirt
     made of spinach
saturday I keep the sabbath and at least
     seven out of the ten commandments
sunday I dress like a mini-mall,
     which means I wear a yogurt hat
     and my shirt is made out
     of 7/11 bags and there
     is the inevitable laundromat tag
     around my neck like a steady ring.

I work there to make ends meet
     my ends don't even meet, get close,
     get married or nothing
     my ends aren't even acquainted
     on a first name basis.

I am paid the minimum wage
and lots of money is taken
out of my paper airplane paycheck
cause george bush thinks the minimum wage
is too high and subversives like me
might spend money buying groceries.
i've had weeks where toothpaste on crackers
was both meal and hygiene.
this while aaron spelling builds his
800,000 square foot home for two.
the murder of robin hood remains unsolved.

being the only employee has its moments
the league of athletics for
macrobiotic record stores
disqualified me saying there is no way
I can be shortstop, pitcher,
cotton candy hawker and left fielder
I said yes yes more more
i'm a liberal
and I saw tom waits playing babe ruth
playing w.c. fields in a movie once
it can be done.

needless to say my team made
the solitaire finals.

people tell me i'm modest but I have a
thriving xylophone making thing going.
in some circles i'm known as the
les paul of the xylophone.
granted I haven't sold any
but not cause they're atonal.

the true reason was a jealous accordion
        player with a john wayne fetish saw me
        picketing his star on hollyhype boulevard
        screaming
        "custer died for your sins"
        and "pow wow power."
a xylophone maker has to follow her heart.
I recognize woodstock nation.
anarchist nation.
sovereign nations.
and I recognize the state of kansas
        from an airplane.

so that's a typical day for me,
at night I look at teabags till i'm drowsy
my stove was repossessed
        so I can't cook no more
but i'm keeping a stiff upper lip
        there's hope.
someone brought a victrola record player
        into the store and the boss of
        employee-pats-on-the-back-every-time-
        i-get-that-i'm-about-to-get-a-real-job-
        selling-kazoos-look hands me that
        mystic, almost dinosaur-wise l.p. dog and
        says a counterfeit penny for your thoughts.
I smile as the victrola dog gives me
        the victory sign.
he has something up his paw.
it looks like revolution from here.
I swear this dog has che guevara's chin.
someday our song will be played.

I GO A LITTLE CRAZY

I go a little crazy
    as it gets closer
    to Valentine's Day

Cupid's Geiger Counter
    spins volcanos
    through my hair
    like yodeling
    for water now
    will have the same effect
    as screaming Noam Chomsky
    in a crowded theater.

EYELID DEEP

I've been eyelid deep in velcro gardens
    like Beckett with a tractor
    and some quicksand
    sticking to soil that was manufactured
    by patent thieves whose feet
    scrape the sound of dragons
    from a clef note's grin.

People held saltshakers full of tourniquets
    with a little vitamin paste in the center
    claiming it was the garlic of now
    to keep one's illusions healthy
    while someone held the smelling salt
    on a ladder, rising like a biblical
    circus trick 'til what was supposed
    to awaken turned to broken aromatherapy
    that played the smells backwards
    and caused mass hysteria.

Billboards shouted in haikus of poison.

Someone sold the pen that dripped magic.

Someone waxed eloquent with a liar's tongue
    poking stigmata in cheek
    the pen was not mourned, eulogized
    or put on milk bottles
    instead, the pen found itself
    in a pencil sharpener
    where it wept baffled ink

flooding the fax machine
causing blurred prayers
and homages to the loneliness
of the long distance facsimile
and into an Internet machine
that said dot com so fast
it started to sound
like numb
like coma
like commandment.

In the fluorescent mausoleum
where flowers lose their petals
the pen was held by someone having
an idea of something so different
they couldn't even whisper it
into their own ear
all they could do was fold the pen
into a fancy lasso shape
like a rodeo of sawhorses and unicorns.

Then the pen dropped into a piece of light
forming a candle.

Someone's voice twirled in the wax museum
as the people put on armor
as they went through the spin cycle
turning lead into blood
and ink into Rorschach
as the bells clang in the skywriting
that the neon ostriches cluck warnings
against looking directly into
like an eclipse for the mind's decay.

Couch potatoes start new famines
and it's a permanent clock
in 1916 Ireland
and 1930's Germany
Always Pine Ridge.

The hotel clocks, instead of having
the time zones of the world,
should instead
tell the time
and how we're the zoned.

The air knows
when it punches its oxygen
at the streams of people
caught in history's headlights

shivering with t.v.
shaking with alcohol rubbed
3rd degree on rugburns
in the infinite crawl
to the sofa, the job
the bed.

The eyes that look out
from steel-tipped houses
and throw shadows
like a banana peel at a movie
too many slip silently on
thinking a chiropractor
will wipe the conscience gone
with the rings of crumbs that promise
with the biggest beaks ever

we'll find our way home.

The fairy tale eaters
    chomp good and melodic
    on peoples' futures
    and make tense proclamations
    with megaphones full of nostalgia
    and see through ghosts
    for the ones wearing glasses
    all over like a dress
    made for an eternal opera

    these glasses are given out at birth
    in the invisible birth canal
    every moment is

    but the people selling vaseline
    and blindfolds
    who tear at the sun
    to give it to the dungeonmakers
    are given everywhere
    to peddle their wares.

WANT TO BE A STRIPPER

Want to be a stripper
Want to sell something
Want to travel

I thought of being a stripper
a girl came into an open mike
and said how she used to be a stripper
it was humiliating
men are jerks to the 100th power
they made us feel like objects she said
I thought that sounds like my life
it sounds like woman's life

our clothes come off in other eyes
why won't that one talk to you
why won't that one sing a song for you

likes your clothes
likes your mind

strip so someone else can know you
strip so you can know yourself

$150 dollars a night
      on a slow night
as a woman you're always on display

$4.25 an hour
you walk cross the street
a man shouts hey fat girl

he strips your mind
strip mining for ladders to climb
    to ejaculate his ego
the land won't be the same

stripping for yourself
putting on Neil Young records
writing a manifesto
life is a nudist camp
    if you're perceptive
you can pretty much tell
    where things stand

where are the callouses of love?
practice living long enough
    and you might get callouses
yet you might not

where does language end and truth begin?
he mentioned illusion
he mentioned reality
he mentioned the past the present
    and the future
he talked with a coyote tongue
he held me with one finger clinging
    to the edge of a cliff

he fell first in my eyes
he fell second in my mind

I wanted to pull him up to solid ground
maybe not entirely solid
maybe baying with tie-dyed alligators
    made his voice sound so smooth

I thought his teeth were
        full of light and mirrors
I wanted to see
        what I wanted to be there
he said we can't...
        to whatever the question was
he said the earth is our mother
I heard him say that

he is holier than a piece of wafer
he is holier than a dreydel
he is holier than an ashram

he won't let you forget
        who he is
he has the power
        to wet your underwear
        make you oversleep
        make your tears run races
        make you go crazy
        crazier than it might have gone
        if you hadn't met

he's well respected
a sage with a hard philosophy

he's on a tangent about 500 years
he's making so much sense
        my mind is in orgasm

simultaneous kindred spirits
hell this ain't easy
genetic memory he says
genetic just like crazy we live to survive

we are
you are
we are
you are
I am .
you are

I am, I said, fed up with your hypocrisy
your genetic memory is Caligula
your genetic raincoat is Pinocchio
you're fooling almost everyone
        almost all the time
they ought to create a museum for you

yes, wow, a girl can't avoid
        being a stripper
        paying a price
        receiving something in her underwear
        or receiving something in her mind
her heart a heart
        searching for callouses
        always a mile ahead of her
        in some corporate conference room

she doesn't really want the callouses
        as much as she wants
        to be understood
        93 percent of the time

she wants to be an astronaut
she feels like she's in a different world
        most of the time

she wants to be a woman
    in a world where history
    and herstory have an equal chance,
    where people realize the sacredness
    of a callous and lack thereof
    the trouble of obtaining a passport
    for a heavier than baggage requirement mind

Yes the women are stripping
Yes they're shedding new skin
Yes the women.

HOW I BECAME A RECORD COLLECTOR

yeah
it started when I found my body kissing yours
    and you said it's our one time together
    and you told me about two different worlds,
    instantly I began the inner pain
    of touching myself nights
    mingled with water and the words
    of the Janis Ian song *Society's Child*
    "baby I can't see you anymore"

my own contribution
    to breaking through to the other side
    stagnated!
we wanted to come together
we wanted each other
the want was wrong
the want was a mistake.

vote here
live here
you have rights here
fuck make love with each other here
we might decide to lynch you here
oh America, you idolize tanning machines
    but what you do to Indians,
    Blacks, and Mexicans
declarations of intolerance
    leave their dust & other violent times
spittle on lips that say
    we the people like woman's hair long
    and man's hair short.

when I heard *Society's Child* on the radio
    it had the kind of impact
    Lather by Jefferson Airplane had
    so very much truth. AM-FM mantra
    good for solitude of the no-prom
    post-adolescent hours in California
    where it's way too easy (& trendy)
    to be hard.

I mean UC Berkeley has banned
    the Grateful Dead
where is the tie-dyed heart?
Cody's Bookstore on Telegraph Avenue
    sits back from the curb
    so the spiritual kids of Mario Savio,
    John Lennon and other philosophers
    can speakeasy.

there's a place for people
    who need to be somewhere
People's Park is the real
    Statue of Liberty.

needing comfort in orifices, crevices,
    ears, eyes, nose and throat
    I went in search of the song.

got close to finding it
a friend spotted it
didn't have the bread to buy it
when I got there — gone.

sold to another horny human
    deprived of true love
    or at least true something.

I decided I'd better continue
    looking more & more
    had gotten so close
I saw records everywhere
    and was vulnerable for
    music to rub up against
    cause your hands weren't
    exploring me no more.

I found *Highway 61 Revisited*
    with my thumb praying in the
    synagogue of an open road
could we knock down the walls
    and call it peace?
could I hitchhike rides to your soul?
do ya still think about me?

liner notes on Dylan albums
    remind me of my Bas Mitzvah
my birthday falls into your mouth
you suck on it
    and I grow older.

yeah, sometimes I wish I had gotten pregnant
    instead of remaining a virgin
    that's my erotic hindsight
    my vision is extreme.

eating quirky
refined sugars
trying to outrun
    the organic screams
my heart melted into scars.

I ate to lose whatever made you want me
my self esteem twirled in the void
realizing I was fat when we met
    and in your eyes I saw completeness
    and sensual intensity
    from the first look.

Society's Child
instant
not new and not improved
we were Romeo & Juliet, Tony & Maria,
West Side Story in the four directions
culture shock warriors
shocking each other the most.

me in the record bins at Bebop,
    at Moby Disc, at Record Surplus,
    with no money and a few orgasms
    as I leaned into an old Blind Faith album.
    hard and soft
    emotions so ethereal
    so like origami
    they can rip.

saw a Leonard Cohen album
some Randy Newman stuff
    I didn't even know existed
first heard of him when I housesat
    for a bird in New York City
how appropriate.

it was such a relief being in
    these real record stores
    after my on call job hours
    as an exploited minimum wage worker
    for a non-record store record store
nintendo — what an eyesore.
I found various Joan Baez albums,
got the soundtrack to *Hair*
Loudon Wainwright III *Unrequited*
Buffy St. Marie
She Used to Want to be a Ballerina
George Harrison *All Things Must Pass*
all sorts of personal notes
    on the record jackets
    sort of a used record chain letter:
    hope you enjoy kiddo
    see you on Thanksgiving
    dig neon but be free
    keep grinning, be.

you gotta wonder in a way when
    you see something inscribed
    dear beloved my love
    why they'd ever get rid of it
hearts change.

at 2:30 A.M. and other circumstances,
    I'm so craved for love
    I kept a card so generic
    it wasn't even to me
    but I respected it
    as performance art
found it in the brim of a hat.

my record collection swells
    along with my memories
you and I were gonna change the world
I still believe maybe we can
    slow the war down enough
    to jump safely to another train.
with your guru teeth
    and my spinster idealism
I'll never completely give up hope.

meanwhile I'm still a virgin
two days after us
    at a poetry reading
    someone said
    you're not a virgin anymore
    you got a look in your eyes
that's the magic you've left me with.

only I thought if I kept my virginity
    I'd keep my sanity
how wrong!
my first sorta time.

Where do I put the records?
I'm getting into 8 track tape.
The world seems to be
    getting into compact disc
    but the world is not compact and simple
    because songs like *Society's Child*
    must be written in 1966 and
    searched for in 1989 for life.

THE DYSFUNCTIONAL SECULAR SERENITY PRAYER

He's like a new type of cramp.
Before I see him I get angry and blue.
I get purple and soft spoken.
I get giddy.
Musical notes walk out of my eyes.
Popcorn for eardrums.
Crushed by the words.
Sifting butter through my mind
    till I'm slippery with forgiveness.
My presence to see
    if I can elicit an emotion
    and you look around me
    you look through me
    above me
    below me
you used to look at me.

This is the country of avoidance
    where flesh is rule.
New anthem of sighs.

I'm listening to Randy Newman
    do a rap song.
My heart is wrapped around your waist
    and I don't know where you are.

My face is too weird for your rock.
My rolls of everything
    is not what you wanted to 33 1/3 in.
Who am I not kidding?

Just playing harmonica
    with my mind
    in a room
    full of walls
    I'm learning to stand up on.

I hardly ever notice the walls these days
    except the big wall that looks like you.
I see the cigarettes and the tennis shoes,
    you're off and running
    like a wild horse with a cough.
Sometimes you need some sugar
    and some taking care of
    but then you throw off the rider.
I did somersaults off the couch.
You felt my trembling.
Yes I didn't want to open my eyes
    and see the magic was real
    but I couldn't control it.

I wanted to feed the zoo of my body
    without losing my mind.
I wanted to stay in your city
    even if there were some
    inconveniences underground.
After all, there was plenty of electricity
there was plenty of light
sockets of bluntness
ceilings of vagueness

I was never going to get no mail
no phone calls
no acknowledgment
I was going to be lost in you
lost in your image

I was going to be small
I was going to quit existing
Except when you needed something
        I couldn't give.
I'd be a scapegoat
        so you could run off to some other.
You were afraid I didn't understand
        the reality.
I was afraid you didn't understand me.

I would be in a lousy relationship.
I'd be like the rest of America,
        unable to trust the other gender.
I'd start to hate you and then
        I'd start to hate your brother.
I'd feel at war.
I'd feel lonely.
I'd cry and start listening to AM radio.
I'd start washing my hands with Palmolive
        thinking then you'd love me
        then you'd wipe my cheek tenderly
        then you wouldn't cheat
        at the real game of poker.
I'd notice my wrinkles,
I was getting old.
If you're fat, men treat you
        as though you're old,
        which tells a lot about the attitude
        to elders this society has.

There's a poem for everything
        for being too depressed to get out of bed
        a poem for love gone wrong
        for love never come
        for unrequited history

between the margins of a poem
    we live
between a record and the liner notes
    our dreams gasp.

He pinched the edge of my hope.
I thought that meant something.
Not just that I was hopeful.

Abundant with wonder
    and then nothing
I've been trying to see
    I have as much right to self-esteem
    as anybody else.
I am not numb.
I just kept stepping on a mirror
    and the shards said figure out
    what's the talk
    and what's the walk,
    don't tumble in between
    the mean and the awful.

I felt the rattle of a punk song
    in my veins, but I bit my lips
    and painted a picture with the blood.

Some utopia near my wisdom teeth.
Some volcano near my molars.
Somebody said don't you think
    you should get health insurance.
I said there is no insurance truly.

He wanted to write the scoreboard
    with my menstrual blood.
He wanted to open my mind
    and pour in cynicism.
He wanted to eat breakfast somewhere else.
It's hard to digest in a room that's spinning
    from disappointment
    from intensity plural
    from games
Lots of resistance took the room
    by surprise.
This didn't happen to hot pieces of ego
    like him.

This room had a way of traveling to Zo
    (the backward land of Oz)
    weird stuff happens there
    if you think Oz was something.

We didn't see a scarecrow.
We didn't see a tinman.
We didn't see a witch.
We became all of the above.

In this land Krishnamurti was the wizard.
The noitutitsnoc (constitution backward)
    was written by Michael Ventura.
The newest bill of right
    was patriarchy was wrong
and bumperstickers saying
    men have given men a bad name
    were everywhere.

This was a place where people came to heal.
People at war went to kiss and make up.
People came here to change.

Things were so dramatically different here
       that when you left
       there were no laws to follow
       no need for any
       in fact the only law was
       at some time you needed to come here.

People are up in arms
       about politically correct
       but what about humanly correct
       equality correct?
There is some commonality in these basics.
Oh yes. Come here.

People were lured with the look of hate
       in their mind's eye
Whooshed here to the land of Zo.
Tofu served 24 hours.
Debbie Gibson music played an hour a day
       to remind you of home.
All the cars have long distance ghosts
       chauffeuring.

You don't need money.
You just need to be willing to love.
Gratuitously. Freely.
The only sacred face in the deck is hearts.
Spades.
Diamonds.
Past ignorance.
Clubs keep love hidden
       for only a certain kind.
We play cards all life long.

You're plunged directly into
　　what you despise.
If you drive a truck
　　with mudflaps glowing in smugness
　　the phrase *No Fat Chicks*
　　you go to a room
　　where Kate Smith is singing
　　and see the beauty in her conviction.
You meet a wallflower at a party
　　who hands you a rose
　　cause you're taking a chance
　　on becoming human.
Not just a man.
A woman who sees a man with glasses
　　as ugly and impotent
　　walks into an eyeglass store
　　and feels the energy of sight
　　as a blind man cries
　　who will love me?

People change quickly.
Everything is heightened.
Attitudes and trends are boycotted.

Sorry is the name of the planet.
Zo is the name of the place.
Sorry has its limits
　　until the pronoun I'm is added.
Try it sometime.
You might see new time dance on your mind.

HE KISSES GIRLS JUST CAUSE THEY'RE BLOND

He kisses girls just cause
    they're blond
    because he knows I have brown hair.
Another kisses girls just cause
    they're blond
    because he's considered
    an outlaw in his culture.
Another kisses girls just cause
    they're blond
    because it will make
    his father jealous.
Another kisses girls just cause
    they're blond
    because she wants to start over.
Another kisses girls just cause
    they're blond
    because T.V. told him
    that would make him happy.
Another kisses girls just cause
    they're blond
    because he says the desperation
    in their eyes is so loud
    he becomes wet.
Another kisses girls just cause
    they're blond
    because he's overweight
    and this makes him feel thin.

Sometimes I feel sorry for blond girls
    as I stand alone
    and kiss myself.

I HAD THE BEST YOGURT OF MY LIFE
IN BERKELEY

I had the best yogurt of my life
    in berkeley.
my tastebuds must be
    socially conscious left wing leaflet
    save the whales and the earth
    old scratchy woody guthrie manifestos
    and static radio simulations
    of buddhist kisses.
I paid 59¢ for that yogurt.
crunchy peanut butter
    with unlimited samples.
it took about twenty minutes to decide.

telegraph avenue.
this is the dawning of the age of
    non-fat yogurt
    non-fat politics
    non-fat homeless
    non-fat demonstrations

the bubblelady blew images around
    cody's bookstore.
the ghost of every unknown poet
    talks in 78 speed to every
    fetal juiced sidewalk stay-putter,
    giraffes wearing bandanas saying
    "free something",
    bobby darin with his lips around
    mack the knife comes out of
    rock a dubdub records,
    this is the version
    most couples make love to.

a man plays chess by himself in the street
spittle leaps from his chin like traffic
        as he wins his fingernail back
his trousers are shaped in fire hydrant
        patterns from leaning 56 hours.

there's a parade of acid rain imported from
        a couple of republican administrassholes.
why do all politicians buy their head gear
        at the general custer salvation store.
it's fishing season and the police and
        hunters are gonna keep shooting native
        americans embracing fish.
why don't you quit your formica salary
        your dress for success furs
        and mercedes (thinking that is the peace
        symbol on the hood of your car)

hey it's night time wake up.
put your pajamas away for awhile.
I'll meet you in berkeley.
I'll meet you in russia.
I'll meet you in israel.
I'll meet you in the place
        between your walkman new age
        relaxation tapes and your channeled entities
        home illusion network

(give me some eye contact)
did I tell you
        the best yogurt I ever had was 59¢
        and the only food I could afford all week.

SCIENCE POEM

I started thinking about
    the wonder of words.

I've always been a good speller
    but I thought a second
    about how science sounded.

I knew it was s-c-i-e-n-c-e
    but it sounded sigh—ence
    or even psy—ence

And I thought wow maybe if people
    looked at the psychological impact
    of inventing cause isn't science
    sort of making known what's here
    in some other form and combining,
    inventing the new fresh
    or the old fresh?

And a sigh, a thoughtful responsible
    pondering sigh, might create a whole
    new outlook for science.

I think science is the microcosm of the
    human spirit.

People probably felt the psychological bomb
    inside their heads, inside their hearts
    caused by maybe bad uncaring parents
    or not being invited to dance
    or what not, before they could
    invent the bomb that kills
    inward and outward and leaves
    buildings unharmed.

I've heard about the guilt of scientists,
        I haven't heard too much about
        the guilt of politicians.

Inventions are sort of weird,
        many take us far away from being human
        Like bosses.

I mean it sort of takes the
        "all men are created equal" thing
        and where is the woman in that
        and says o.k. you're created equal
        but at the moment of conception
        it's the bosses and the
        who will be bossed
        the haves and the have nots, etc.

Science is the invention of a weight scale
        a machine with numbers that
        turns people crazy, tears at self-esteem
        but is it the numbers
        or the people that serve
        as mean weight guessers
        at the carnival of planet earth.

Now science is not all bad,
        not by a long shot,
        if it weren't for phonograph
        I wouldn't be able to hear
        Idiot Wind by Bob Dylan unless
        I went to a concert
        and he felt like doing it
        and who knows.

If it weren't for science
　　　I couldn't stay up day and night
　　　listening to KPFK.

So science has many good things going
　　　it's how it's used.

Science is as vulnerable as
　　　any other human thing.

It's supply and demand.

If the people look like they're going
　　　to be having a war, war toys
　　　and war bumperstickers and
　　　other stuff will be invented.

On the other hand, people will rise
　　　with poetry and songs and wisdom
　　　to tilt back the world.

Unfortunately, ego gets in the way.
Science says, wow!
　　　that is such a fantastic television set
　　　but I can make a bigger better T.V. set
　　　than that scientist with the masters' degree
　　　plus my T.V. set will have a swimming pool inside
　　　and be fluent in 39 languages.

And this T.V. will make me famous
　　　I'll be on T.V.

And one person
    the richest person in the world
    buys the T.V. and he is the only one
    who can afford this "miracle."

And he decides to invite one person over
    to watch some documentaries.

And this one person is starving
    because she thinks the richest man
    will like her cause she's thin.

So when a commercial comes on for soup
    she rubs her hand against the screen
    thinking this magic machine
    will feed her.

The man slaps her for getting fingerprints
    on the screen and so she gets up
    too desperate to leave cause
    if he's so rich
    he must be the best man.

So she realizes this T.V. has a bunk bed
    so she lays inside the T.V.
        trying to sleep but the man says
        your breasts are making
        a shadow on the screen
        and she vows to eat less
        than nothing tomorrow.

So she says
    this machine doesn't give food
    doesn't give shelter
    what does it give?

He said
> it gives me an excuse
> to pretend you're not there.

And she walked slowly to the pool part
> of the T.V. set and kept walking.

And he flipped channels
> thinking he could escape life by UHF.

But the woman was swimming on T.V. now.

She was famous.
He was rich.
Drowning in different water.

They didn't have anything they needed,
> lots of people told them
> they had it all.

I hear these T.V. sets
> have become affordable now.

FIDO

fido wrote a screenplay
fido wrote me into the screenplay
fido is a sensitive dog
yes. he is a dog
he is a dog in that he has
    four legs and not two
    a tail
    and bad odor mouth.

I keep fido's things organized
fido's things
    are rulers, yarn
    and bourbon crackers.

fido is a well read dog
fido reads kafka
he reads aloud
    and I type
    curtains to the windows.
he keeps milkman hours
    and drinks orange juice
    with lemon.

newspapers written in velcro
    line the tables.
fido picks and hunts
    at the feature articles
    looking for the who, what, when,
    where and how
    of a particular moment.

fido is a perceptive dog
        and I type slowly.
california is his hometown
he's lived here only 8 years
        but he's deeply in debt
        and likes magic marker
        and water
        on his notepad.
he uses pens
        and uses them 'til they're dry
        and dips them in water.

fido drives an automatic sled
        compromising on his ancestors
        who were eskimo pull dogs.
he has that indigenous "woof"
        in him and reads a lot of
        native american poetry
        as he faces the four winds
        to stay in touch.

fido has never been a popular dog
        but the other dogs respect him.
he wasn't always a screenplay writer,
used to lecture in front of van gogh's
        paintings on the meaning of crows
        in pre-1900 amsterdam.
avoiding pretension, fido made a lot of
        contacts and was asked to write a movie
        about andy warhol's left eye.
that started fido.

3000 pages later
    he was a known commodity
    and was paged regularly at club lingerie
    where he tied the drummer's shoelaces
    together during cover versions of
    stairway to heaven.
it was only minutes
    before he had his own
    fire hydrant at spagos
    and not near the clatter of the kitchen
    like rin tin tin.
fido was living.
his heartbeat an infinite bow wow wowie.

I am a groupie, I admit it.
i'm not in it for the sex
    though I have these fantasies
    we do it in a doghouse.
we are platonic.
he doesn't see through me.
just the mention of rabies shots
    makes me horny.
I am sick. yes but I realize it.

I type 80 hangnails a minute
    with long rolls of paper
    jack kerouac style
    part of the dialogue
    (the character actor part)
    I type on a fringed vest
    the ingenue words I sew onto a mini-gown
    that ran away from paris 5 times
    and got it right,

we built a wardrobe
and took meetings with
other precocious fabric.
that was hollywood.
it was a bow eat bow world.
our production company was called
cannibals over the parties begun i.n.c.

his parents only now are beginning
to talk with fido.
his mom wanted him to live
a responsible life
her hopes were for him to be
a guide dog for the blind
or at least a dog who kept
the cattle together on a farm
in upstate upstate holding
the idealistic value system together.

fido had other ideas in mind.
he dreamt in panshots and chromakey
and it's a wrap.
fido wanted to direct but most of all
fido wanted to be a poet.
he'd snicker as the other dogs
would laugh at him
saying "I only am doing this
so I can have enough flow
to write the great poem."

he wasn't a hack.
he took great care and wrote
his scripts 300 times if need be.

I know, I typed each page backwards,
forwards, in aboriginal tongue,
and while pink floyd music played
and blared simultaneously
in the room one room away.

fido sang and wrote the music
      for every screenplay.
he was the danny elfman of labradors.

he didn't always chow at spagos.
when he stood up for
      better working hours for neuters
      he was roughed up by a couple
      of german shepherds with poodle masks
      bought on melrose.
fido is in the spirit of an activist.
he reads the bible, grew up in berkeley
      and practices civil disobedience
      at obedience schools.

that's when his father threw shoes at him
      and fido left home
a stronger dog
a lonely dog
no more certain frisbees to catch
      in people's park.

he hitchhiked on an 18 wheel cheese truck
      with a chain smoking bowling champion.
they compared life stories and fido was
      dropped off in st. louis
      where he managed a comedy club
      called purple glue.

between sets fido kept up
   a stream of jimi hendrix songs
   playing for the chairs and the ashtrays.

after about 29 hours, a hearse owned by a
   post hippie flower sniffing butterfly
   seduced fido into giving the
   hollywood sign a chance.
he took an ashtray and the
   letter Z off the marquee
   and didn't sleep for seven winters.

he waited on tables
   in vegetarian neighborhoods.
he soothed the rioters who claimed
   dog would be tasty.
he bought a compact disc player.
he had a record player
   and loved mono-sound on his
   rock and jazz but the victrola dog
   reminded him of an upper pedigree
   who had kept him out of the restricted
   white collar and leash club
   a fugue oriented classical music
   organization for sadistic chihuahuas.

fido met me when I answered an ad
   for girl wednesday
it was tuesday
   and I had nothing better to do
the ad said spacious mind
   and cluttered xylophone doodler seeks
   dreamer with tiptoes on the ground.

I was wearing platform heels
    and singing the collected hits
    of shel silverstein, abba and jung
    and felt what I had left to lose
    was lost itself — I got the job.

fido writes screenplays.
he doesn't know I love him.
I must have a paw fetish.
canine film festival is next week
    and I might tell him I have feelings
    of a planets colliding
    over reacting nature
    but he'll just growl at me
    and sing "i'm the kind of dog
    who likes to run around blah blah blah"
fido is a successful dog
soon he's going to be wanting telex
    and call waiting on the phone
he is sensible
he is stubborn

fido collects fine art
    and then rips the picture
    off the frame.
he says he can't stand waiting in line
    at art mart to get canvas
    and by the time he carries it home
    on his sled in gridlock traffic
    he loses the idea.

fido is an artist
I think he remembers what it's like
    to be a starving museum talker.

he's written 83 screenplays.
had 800 conversations with agents.
his hands air harmonicas
        as he convinces them he won't sell out
        and put on turtleneck music.

one of these days fido will write
        poetry with two hands.
I think he's trying to prove something
        to his parents still.
they have their own barbara woodhouse video
        at the veterinarian's summer home.
they live good but they still point
        at the beagle, stan, who is a chiropractor
        in new hampshire and his sardines in a can
        crowded fluorescent expensive view office.
there will always be backs misspent on
        piano lessons and swimming.
there will also be dogs who have to trust
        their next meeting will actually reveal
        more than clotted dollar bills
        but passion.

some dogs will never please their parents.
I pray fido will at least be able
        to please himself.
if not the left brain.
than at least the other.

meanwhile I hear the crumpling of sunlight
        and fido needs his under ears scratched.

another raymond chandler moon rises
        and fido hands me a piece of linen
        and tells me to go.

I leave now and so glad because
        only alone will he write that damn poem.

besides, I put 2 dabs of perfume
        in his dish.
I marked my territory.
fido knows
        if you have 50¢ to buy a duplicate key
        you can go home again.

CHROMAKEY CHORDS

There are divers who cut their hearts open
    from the seashells
    and the visions of starfish
    bearing bottles full of messages
    and souvenirs.

I heard 130 seconds of Stan Ridgway's
    concert at Tower Records.

Traffic named the snail
    its animal of the year
    and we celebrated accordingly.

I ran into the store and he was singing
    while wearing a hat of many noirs.

I tiptoed on my ballerina adrenaline
    past the top 5 albums
    the top 5 campaign promises
    the top 5 books proclaiming
    the Internet should win the Nobel,
    Pulitzer, Peace and Crackerjack box prize.

I looked at the billboards
    screaming "Impeach Denial."

I saw harmonica clouds
    in the fluorescent sky.

I saw love beads levitating
    from the microphone.

I saw endorphins dwelling
    in the house of the
    sublime record collection.
I was rubbing my eyes
    and hearing a philosophical cocktail.

80 senses rushing my core like an apple
    touched by an organic garden
    kiddie corner from
    Krishnamurti's oak tree.

There was an IMAX screen selling popcorn
    to this larger than life celebration
    trauma minute and a half of everything.

Edward R. Murrow whispered in my brain
    you are there back in the Troubadour
    you are there back at the Free Press
    you are there being ensconced
    in a feud with Dylan
    you are there
    singing of crystal palaces
    swinging off the rafters

    not hanging from them.

There are optical illusions in life,
    like in science class.
    the old woman sees a gray hair
    from one direction
    and the cook sees a hair in the soup
    from another.

The history of Phil Ochs
     ran through my bones
     as I watched the performance.

I felt the Pentagon rise
     with the taste of earth in its mouth.
I felt the megaphone of Mario Savio
     in your vowels and larynx of gold.

I saw the founding of a country
     with no marching
     not now
     not ever
     not nowhere

I saw the grace
     said before true nourishment.

The landscape danced
     in your Kurt Weill meets gravity voice.

Welcome mats to the world of Ridgway
     blared a melodious ode to the ceiling
     and its murals of time.

H.G. Wells annointed me
     a time traveler
     or was it something I was born with?

I heard for every second of your song
     a medley of
     Love Me, I'm A Liberal
     The Doll House
     The World Began In Eden and
     Ended In Los Angeles

Like a speaker that picks up
      Nebraska, Oregon
      New York and Amsterdam
      while in Switzerland.
It was cosmopolitan grief.

It was a collision of joy and pain.

This has more to do with me than you
      more to do with me than
      all the zines at Tower
      more to do with me than
      all the identification needed
      to check in a bag of miracles
      at the curtain magic marked memory.

20 years ago Phil Ochs died
7 years ago Abbie Hoffman
12 years ago Richard Brautigan

They painted their masterpieces
      in the collective fingerpaint
      of the era in which they lived.

I woke up screaming for months
      after Abbie's death.
Once at a talk he gave
      someone mistook me for his child
      and in the simple coincidence
      I found a home in the water
      he helped give health to
      in upstate New York
      with leaflets and oxygen.

Richard Brautigan dances into all my reasons
        why I have more library cards
        than credit cards
        more chapbooks
        than hardcovers.
Why the dewey decimal system
        will never fully be decimated
        in a country fighting
        to tear apart the alphabet.

Phil Ochs whose stiff upper lip
        intonation of Dylan
        spoke to the whimsical
        and bitter love child
        in us all.

I laughed at the inside outside joke
        of that Dylan put-on
        accentuating the real,
        then I cried.

The heartbreak of Joan Baez
        in her version of
        Love Is Just A 4 Letter Word
        with Dylan tongue linguistics
        is a constitution for
        everybody touched by love
        and its fleeting rainbow storm.

Phil Ochs with the delicacy of origami
        and the wishbone pulled apart by
        a topical magnifying 20/20 vision.

Broken wishbones
        are a big cause of destruction.

Highest cause of death
　　downwind of certain mindsets.

The continual flurry of butterflies flapping

　　against dollar bills
　　against grenades
　　against orchards

　　with all the one bad apples
　　in the bunch joined together
　　and called

　　sometimes war
　　sometimes America
　　sometimes life

I was listening to Phil Ochs'
　　Rehearsals for Retirement
　　and each note made me cry.

I was wearing my heart a cappella
　　on my sleeve,
　　my face contorted in the opera
　　of many things I wish I could change.

When Side B was to begin
　　there was this pause
　　that sounded like
　　the moon that told the astronauts
　　I'm tired of footprints.

The tape was rolling
　　but the sound was
　　not in the universe.

I ran to the radio
 my tears cupped in my eyes
 like nuts hibernating
 for the long stream of sandcastles
 driven down by rent gone amok.

The tape strand was gone
 not eaten up
 not wrinkled
 not being ironed
 by Bob Dylan
 like Joan Baez's hair in one of
 the cutest pictures of togetherness
 in a world of solitaire.
Not even resting in the leader.
Just vanished.

the songs lingering
 like a map from the womb.

Somewhere there is a band playing
 the biggest big band of all
 consisting of everybody's idea
 of a beat by a different drummer.

And radio shies away from that drum
 as they shy away from the drums
 that accompanied the sound of birth
 and the sound of hieroglyphics
 and the sound of sound
 within a well.

Joan of Arc played those different drums
 that instrument nobody wants to endorse
 the price is too high.

Yet the thump of music
        scorches the world
        when all that is left
        is charred soundbites.

I wanted to grab so many legs as they entered
        the guillotines of their psyches
        as the quicksand blew their doubts around.

I wanted and wanted and wanted
        and I'm left with the spoon
        the archaeology
        the bones of song

        the songs that are
        the last piece of dust
        that will leave the earth
        no matter how hard
        we spin on our axis.

I'M NOT HUNGRY LIKE THAT

I'm not hungry like that.
I can't forget miss jane pittman like that.
at least three times a year on television
tasting water from a white bubbler.
cicely tyson made up to look 114 years old.
miss jane pittman on t.v.
look ma, come and watch t.v., mom.
I looked forward to it
    like I did "girl most likely to"
    stockard channing ugly mallard duckling
    gets plastic surgery
    and blows her teasing classmates away.
I walked into barney's brouhaha
    intent on seeing what this male bonding
    cigarettes under the roof of the throat
    leather jacket stud ritual was all about.
chili, 50,000 different types of chili.
I ate pancakes.
banana flour and banana cut-ups.
andy warhol must have made these pancakes.
neon bananas and day-glo toothpicks
    by a polyester parking lot.
2¢ mints for 15¢

suddenly and I mean suddenly
    like revelation throws a punch
    with hollering penguins on acid
    cold turkeys in heat
I remembered an article I read once.
there was a sign at this eatery
no indians allowed.

my fork slid like rosebud
        in a colorized version of *citizen kane*
        into the chef/owners office.
hell this was 1989.
this was los angeles.
this was a mile away
        from the wild west
        commemorative napkin rodeo.

the maitre 'd wearing a large swastika
        with an eagle through it
        and a swagger in his voice
        and a republican attitude
        started to scream at me
        cause I was sitting there crying.
he said "you liberal slut
        it's the fittest!
        survival for the fucking fittest!
        I don't need a bunch of
        communist indians doing
        red power dances on my almost
        rent controlled affirmative action
        low sodium chili bistro."

it was as though the sawdust mouth
        of general custer spoke.
it was like columbus had discovered
        that america was nothing more
        than a box of crayons
        with red, white, and blue
        in various shades.
I rambled about fishsticks in buffalo sauce.
I rambled about sovereign nations
        and free wisdom.

it's about 1st, 2nd, and 3rd class tickets
on airplanes flying over stolen land
and it's about how many women signed the
declaration of independence
and indians couldn't even vote until
the 20th century.
it's about men only clubs
and the national society for
the advancement of white men coming quickly
to a burned cross at a lynch mob near you.
it's about tree houses that
keep the clumsy out
and clothing stores that don't ask
the overweight girls if they need help
even though they're looking
for necklaces and motivation.

and that's about all I remember
cause the next time I came to
it's 3:30 in the morning
and i'm on the sunset strip.
it's cold enough for the windows to frost
but I see miss jane pittman
the movie credits rolling down her face
with tears of pride and anger
and I feel the pancakes I ate
rushing my stomach like tomatoes
and ice cream dared in hazing weeks
swallowed as 1000 fraternity boys
climb into a telephone booth and
make unsuspecting crank calls to nuns.

and I see all the heads
    of organized religion bejeweled
    in the frocks and old time prejudices
    and boycotting traditional languages
    and the glee of pow wows and warriors
    who need to get a good night's sleep too
    and I see the cheekbones of deserts
    without having to wipe my eyes open.

it's just there.
kaleidoscopes in my bones
    like ink and manifestos.

i'm surprised they let me walk the streets
    and the cops only beat me
    every third day now and that's only
    the volunteer police department.

wait 'til the chief of police gets
    a hold of me but I speak in solidarity
    with chief joseph and crazy horse,
    frida kahlo and malcolm x, joan of arc,
    leonel rugama and helen keller.

I wish sandy koufax could pitch a nine inning
    dinner of sundried tomatoes at this
    better be out of town before sundown cafe

    where the forget me not floral centerpiece
    is the only thing edible.

There is a wall chart that reads: plastic, asbestos,
    sweat and biting one's tongue
    are the four major food groups.

I smell the sizzle from the stakes that are
    home grown and branded USDA
    (United States Deity is Amnesia)

cause this is 1989
cause this is 1984
cause this is 1492

do you dig?

AN ELLYN MAYBE POEM

Sometimes I wish it were about 10 years ago.
I was miserable.
I threw portable fans
    trying to cool off the temperature.
I kicked, punched and screamed.
I beat my head into walls.
I cried when everything else
    was too exhausting and then
    that too consumed my lungs
    and cardiovascular potential.
10 years ago I was still on the cusp
    of meeting my niche
    and the cusp is sometimes just as bad
    as being 10 billion miles away.
So while others had beauty
    and some had grace
    and some had significant history
    and some had dance partners
I got my attention by being a
    she-could-lose-it-at-any-moment caricature
    of a tormented suicidal girl out of time.

It was sincere.
There was little remorse.
Just big remorse.
Cumulative payments.
The rage was so common
    that when anything went calmly
    I was totally elated
    as though I'd better live this joy fully
    before it dissipates again.

This card house was full of kingdoms
        jokers, hearts.
Royalty crowned me and said
        "girl, so much self-pity
        do a little dance, make a little love,
        get down tonight!"
Wasn't that K.C. and the Darkness Band?
        get real!

I looked at suicide hotlines
        like cooks look at recipes,
        knowingly but slightly skeptical.
I tried to go to carnivals
        but the air was too bitter
        with broken laughter.
I thought I needed a 24 hour hospital
        but I needed an almost 24 hour coffeehouse.

When words curled around my mind and said
        please take us in, love us,
        name our language
It gave me a responsibility equal
        to motherhood
        stronger than citizenship
        higher than helium even dreams about.
When I want to throw a piano
        at your song and dance
        dance and song
        cynical prison for pleasure
I instead pick up a pencil.

When I want to fall on my knees
        in front of you and say no,
        I'm not intending on giving you head

I was thinking more along the line
of fairy tales
how 'bout happily ever after
or something slightly more permanent.
But having sympathy for your bare feet
and bifocals, I didn't want to see you
get all out of breath running away
from my sensible soul and wild throat.

So I wrote.
I wanted to tell everybody
watch out women
he just wants your flesh
You could be in my shoes years later
trying to do cartwheels in quicksand.
But some just want his flesh too.
So I brought a notebook with me
to the river in my mind
and dipped my eyes in deep.
There was always now a healthy way
to vent rage.

It made me sick.
I couldn't justify throwing things.
I memorized the names of folk singers
past, present, and get this — future
I couldn't scream
as the walls banged my head.
Some of the polite walls parted
and became doors.
I forgot where
the suicide hot line numbers were.
I stayed up all hours
talking about living.

The words said
    "Mama, we feel pretty safe you'll always
    shelter us
    no abandoning us
    we don't have any connections
    with rent control
    we love you for honoring us."
And every day was Mother's Day
    and being word ma made me even
    more appreciative of my mom
So when I occasionally threw my past at her
    and she ducked
I forgave her
I felt remorse for all of us
The words that were in me for so many years
    waiting to hatch
    waiting for me to say
    I was ready to rise above myself
    and become more myself
    levitating to a different magician
And realizing the people who are
    ashamed of me
    and my quirks
    are not growing
    they are wilting
And I stand ready with water

The ritual is ancient
Wallflower becomes sunflower becomes poet
This stuff is ordinary and extraordinary
Becomes painter
Or incense stick maker
Or archivist
Or card house interior decorator

Sometimes I want to get so close to you
and remember all I ever forgave
and scream in your ear
but I realize
a poem is the scream that lasts

but just to make sure I get through
if in your dreams
you hear a hissing sound,
it's just your conscience or me

Or just history breathing.

NOT YET

My Allen Watts tapes are rewound.
So are my Michael Ventura tapes
        and Helen Caldicott too.
I wrap my ears and heart around
        Pacifica for nourishment.
I'm thinking of painting my car yellow
        and turning it into a bus.
I defend mother earth.
I'll armwrestle for father sky.
I boycott lots and lots of stuff.
I giggled at a crystal in the window
        of a new age bookstore.
I play a guitar made of tofu.
I sang happy birthday to a river.
I gave my teeth goddess names.
I visualized wisdom.
Did you hug an organic farm today?
Has your guru asked
        for your charge card yet?
I changed all the currency
        to pictures of floods, pictures of war,
        drawings of overdoses,
        people with their backs turned.
Money ought to reflect the society
        it has bought.
I took to the road
Stood in front of the Pentagon and asked
Trick or trick or trick or trick

For Halloween I saw how people sank
        as they dunked for survival.
New apples in the garden of toxic waste.

I changed the national anthem to
    My Country Tis of Thy People You're Dying
    by Buffy St. Marie.
I painted a shadow around the White House.
I saw leaders fall into quicksand
    of their ego.
I saw followers breakdown
      then rise with the taste
    of their own strength.
I saw people give the peace sign
      and then use those two fingers
      as a guillotine to cut up hope
      in an embracing heart.
I saw hip.
I saw trendy.
I saw Emperor's New Clothes
    on all the racks.
I saw hypocrisy.
I heard people call ignorance a treat
    as they said to me
    you trick us
    you scare us
    you're a witch
    please shut up.

I said every day is halloween.
And they said
    you're fat
    you don't know
    you are nothing
    you are nothing
    you are nothing but a crazy woman
    you rant and tangent.

And I said what do you see?
And it was as if the earth
    quit breathing to see what
    all its children would mumble.
And the telephones that dialed evangelists.
And the telephones that dialed 976.
And the telephones that dialed dianetics
    fell to a collective snug fit
    on the receiver.

And people with homes ran outside
    and the homeless looked paranoid
    and then facing each other
    saw the differences vanish.
And people said this is something!
The paintbrushes we use may be different.
The thickness of paint may be different.
How far back we stand to see a painting
    may be different.
But each empty canvas has remarkably
    similar space.
It's in knowing humans and flowers
    dance together like lovers
    as do birds and gazelles.

The businessman said "my peace of mind
    cannot be traded for green sandpaper
    with bloody presidential mindsets on it
    no more.
    business as usual is unusual,
    unnatural and unwise."

People shivered and used their
        alarm clocks to not be afraid of time.
And people said "come on let's go"
        nobody asked where.

They all just intuitively split to Washington
        and saw the White House curled in a ball.
        goosebumps of fear scarring the door.
        paint peeling.
And the people said
        "let's kill the bastards."
And someone said
        "that takes us one step closer
        to being them.
        let's just stare as out come those
        skinless robots running
        to the weapon store for
        one last shot of testosterone."

And the people were split.
The non-violent and the almost non-violent
        weren't on speaking terms
        but someone said
        we can't kill the dead
        and we can't bring back the dead.

Someone said that's right
Another one said right on
Someone looked confused

Someone sang
  The People United Will Never Be Defeated
Someone drummed and sang
  the American Indian Movement song
Someone sang *Mary Had A Little Lamb*
Someone sang *We Shall Overcome*
Someone sang *And The Times They Are A Changin'*

Someone said how long do you think
  this will last?
I said it will last as long as it lasts.

BALL & CHAIN RECORD STORE

Someone came into the ball and chain
    record store I work at
    and said no bags
    a waste of plastic.

I said yes.
You must be a granola-eating, left-wing,
    dig-gothic, post-modernist, watch a lot
    of Billy Jack movies, Arlo Guthrie type.

He said yes.
I smiled.
I dream of Tom Waits fingerpainting
    lightbulbs on my holiday wreath
    and I'm Jewish, pretty weird huh?
    I celebrate Tiny Tim's birthday
    with a parade of dancing deadheads
    some who never sleep and some
    who never go to the bathroom.

His T-shirt said have you hugged
    a rainforest today?

I said I love the planet
    but it's unrequited love.

He told me babe, you're bringing me down.
When I was born my first word was ohmmm...

In kindergarten I organized the pacifists
    to demand we didn't have to read
    from Dick, Jane and Spot books.
    Too generic.

I demanded we get American Indians
    to talk about what's real.
And I gave them my nap mat
    cause it's their land and
    I gave them my peanut butter
    and jelly sandwich cause
    the buffalo have been murdered
    and they need protein.

He blushed with passion and said
    tell me you.

Well, the first 15 years of my life
    I thought Barry Manilow was a sex symbol.
Needless to say I got a sort of late start
    at being at one with the cosmic heartbeat.

He gave me one of those looks
    like I better get this girl
    some Jack Kerouac books to read fast
    before she suffers the confusion
    of not knowing there's other existences
    beside the banal.

I put my hands on my hips and squealed
    I read *On The Road*
    and the letters of Allen Ginsberg to Neal Cassady
    and vice versa.

He said on Monday, Wednesday, and Saturday
    I'm a part time Marxist.
He took out a beanie
put it on his head
and began to chant.

This definitely turned me on.
All of a sudden he began to sing
    the minimum wage workers' song
    "the walls are full of faces
    the mini-malls are full of neon
    the bitter bite the hands that feed them
    the food is a mixture of bone, blood
    and snails
    man is a cannibal."

I said wow! you are the sort of guy
    who says right on and really means it.
You probably only drink the milk
    of socially conscious cows
    who voted Crosby, Stills, Nash and Young
    for president.

He screamed, oh chick, my life changed
    in 1962 when I realized the Constitution
    was written without women, blacks,
    indians, and poor white men in mind.
That was not o.k.

I became the Jackson Pollack of feminism.
I threw paint of outrage everywhere.
I was a man who identified
    with Billie Holiday and Ernest Hemingway.
I was a traveler.

So what brings you into this
    San Fernando Valley air conditioned
    intellectually malnourished record store
    with the exactlys?

We open exactly at 10:00
Close exactly at 10:00
No matter what our karma
Damn it's so crass,
      you can't even rent *The Last Waltz* here.

He said I'm in a competitive mantra makers
      bowling league.
We have weavers, chess players,
      avant-garde stamp collectors
      and Hell's Angels.
      Inventors all.
We bowl whenever the fuck
      the spirit moves us.
With any luck we'll be playing the
      New Age/lawyers/used car salesman league
      again real soon.

Hippies and New Age people are like
      the difference between Bob Dylan and Bob Hope.

He smiled and said do you want to bowl?
We are definitely into strikes
      for the betterment of the worker.
We need someone who looks
      like she could walk into the woods
      and find incense without getting poison ivy.
You look like Van Morrison
      when you pout your lips.
You could be a part of the father, son and
      the holy ghost meshuganeh athletic league.
Besides I love you.

I started to weep.
　　　Tears of Bas Mitzvah cake
　　　and tears of being the last kid picked
　　　for field hockey in gym class.
Authentic tears.
Nobody ever said all that to me before.
I guess I kind of do have Van Morrison's mouth.
Why hadn't anybody ever noticed?

I said I love you.
But every free moment I moonlight at
　　　Hairy Krishna Organic Coiffures
　　　and Tea Salon.
We use
　　　no chemicals
　　　no dyes
　　　no sprays
　　　no combs
　　　no brushes
Hell, you look pretty much the same going out
　　　as going in.

He said what's a nice girl like you doing
　　　living in a Republican administration
　　　like this?

The manager of the record store comes over
　　　and says
You know the movie *Fahrenheit 451?*
Corporate has ordered us to burn it.
Get to it!
Don't give me your damn whimpering
　　　Joan of Arc eyes.
Lots of people would love to have your job.

I screamed pig! PIG!
You are giving barnyard animals a bad name.
Cops are Pigs!
Intolerants are Pigs!
Bigots are Pigs!
Everybody who does it and says
     they're just doing their job is a Pig!
Everybody who does it to someone else
     knows what they are.

This is my first day at the record store.
I guess if they want to have a quiet
     complacent yes sir type of employee
     they ought to ask different questions
     on the application.

Like do you conform?
Like do you care that this is stolen land?
Like do you believe in playlists?
Like do you believe in yourself?
Do you mind waking up alone
     rather than being beat up with fists?
Do you see the government is beating us up
     as bad as a knife in our elbows
     as bad as a slur in our ears
     as bad as a rape
     when we just wanted to be held

And all they ask is
     can you work part-time?
     and what days can't you work?
     and they say whom do we contact
     in an emergency?

I said
    cause you need to ask that
    constitutes an emergency.

The hippie said my name is Hell's Bells
    but you can call me hope.
He said I dug you.
Now I dig your whole being.
It's strange,
No matter how many nights I wake up unhappy
    there is still a possibility of rising
    into a change so easily.
The outlaw lives in a world where
    when he sees a mirror he sees a hero.
And all heroes put their bellbottoms on
    one leg at a time.

Let's face it,
How can you trust money when
    there are politicians' faces printed on it.
Money is sexist.
The only woman on so-called American currency
    which is really Turtle Island to the Indians
    is Susan B. Anthony and they stopped making those
    real fast.

Is money worth killing for?
Is money worth dying for?

I ran through the store singing
    about William Blake's eyebrows
    and Walt Whitman's bellybutton
    saying everything is alive
    and everything is sort of adorable.

I took paperclips and gave them
    to loving vegetarian families
    who needed someone.

I took the bathroom sink and gave it a hug.
I freed all the rubberbands!
And I said to all the plastic bags
    I will never burden you
    with films weighing you down,
    Perry Como cassettes,
    or even a piece of Jerry Garcia's beard.
Well maybe.

But I will never staple a bag
    for you brought love.

Most people tell me
    it was all the pop tarts I ate.
Some people tell me
    it was because I was a liar.
And I said I'm too honest
    to be anybody's best friend
But at times nobody believes
    this hippie ever even came by.

There are
    no lingering peace signs
    no incense
    no tea bags
    no fuck the fuckers pamphlets
Yet I still can't even believe
    Abbie Hoffman is dead.
So my strengths and pains
    are in my sense of wonder.

All I know is I don't believe in
     wearing sandals and argyle socks together.
And when I needed it most, hope was here.
Change must not be too far behind.

EARRINGS OF THE TRAIL OF TEARS

it's a country and western bar
    but it sells jewelry and ten gallon
    georgia o'keefe,
you know the skulls of a milk dairy
    new mexico rising cow
    and the jukebox plays the songs
    will sampson most wanted to speak
    about in *one flew over the cuckoo's nest*
in a corner of the table where a man
    was buying fry bread
    enough for a family of three.
I saw it,
a pair of earrings
    and on the package read
    $4.95 trail of tears
    aural/visual/psychedelic
    seashells for the ears
inside every black coral hill
    was a square acre of water
    just the size of the bloodshot eyes
    that had cried in forced relocation
    in massacre
    earrings of all tribes
I opened the earrings with a hair pin
    and wondered if I would be cursed.
my fingernails howled with the chill
    of the earth when somebody listens.
the kids of the flower children
    had good names: parsley, sage, rosemary
    and thyme, moon organic rice, groovy nutmeg,
    hair with part in the center.

these are the names hard to find
     personalized shoelaces for
     in generic toy stores.
it was all paisley burping and tie-dyed rattle.

it's 1989
I was brought back from berkeley
     a flag with an upside down peace symbol.

I wonder if turtles get bitter at having
     their necks hunted down for being
     the collar of artiste bongo haunt smoke
     saxophone jackson pollack modeled fabric.
. it's got to be a drag after awhile.

ticket stubs from woodstock are worth
     (for what it's worth) $18,000 dollars now.
karma for the record store owner
     whose voice eats adrenaline
     when he says no
     we don't carry compact disc
     and we like it that way.
what about the guy who paints eggs
     with zen proverbs in griffith park?
what about the ballerina
     who broke both her hips
     when a cop struck her with his baton
     on the protest line
     and she forgot how to land.

I took a boat ride but being rather poor
     I couldn't afford the boat
     so I called it swimming.

I wore my free peltier pin
        and a george harrison iron-on t-shirt.
it was a left wing lake.
only left handed seagulls
        flew across the sky.

anyway I noticed leonard peltier
        and george harrison
        (in his ravi shankar period)
        looked alike and they both looked like
        frank zappa in the instant
        when he had been told kelloggs
        had just named a cereal after him.

let's go back some thirty years
leonard on the rez
george in liverpool
different same hungers
both wanting to create music

we listen to george with lovers
        and peppermint candles
        and in solitude and fresh card decks
        and 1/2 bite left in a savoy truffle

leonard sits in leavenworth
his eyes going deeper into blindness
his eyes going further in seeing
        what must be seen.

we all have the power of the earth
gurus just have longer goatees
call it a beard
call it a well set jaw

gurus ride bicycles all the time
        in topanga canyon.
leonard gets a benefit concert
        in orange county in his name
        and joni mitchell, kris kristofferson
        and willie nelson are banned on radio
        for giving their time
        while leonard serves his
        in the pitchforks of a couple hundred
        wardens who grew up leaning
        on cigar store indians

        and keystone cops throwing pies
        at crazy horse, geronimo and red cloud
        in a movie clip given a humanitarian grant
        from the general custer bicentennial
        motion picture home archive society.

the richest country ever
        is a cannibal of the spirit.
worshipping a fax machine, avoiding truth.
an eden where only bottled water
        is drinkable.
the rest is tooth rot.
swerving around truth like it is a
        pothole that would chew the tires
        of angry tread and clowns.

leonard
to me you are more real than a documentary.
even a film director says, cut it's a wrap.

these days it's getting harder to know
      who's a revolutionary.
      opening the mouth to scream
      and opening the mouth to yawn
      looks the same eight miles away
      but the air is an opera
      and knows the difference.
I mean people in condos read marx.
trailer park managers have their
      well-thumbed through copies of john reed's
      10 days that shook the world on the porch
      by the fake cactus plant for
      the new prospective tenants to see.

usually at this point somebody tells me
      I'd better go out and buy some steely dan
      and play them at 78 speed.
this is where my head is at.

there is a steven biko song
a nelson mandela song
is there a julius and ethel rosenberg song?

at first having a cricket in the floor boards
      annoys so you say damn
      and buy repellent
      then you change your mind,
      get used to the oppression of the chortled
      windpipe of the sweet insect.
the cricket meanwhile wants to be liberated
      and doesn't realize you think he's caruso
      and are content to let him stay there

provided you can run down to buy your
lotto tickets and aren't too inconvenienced
in a day to night to midnight
rainbow sort of way.

it's like musical prison sentences anyway.
if leonard peltier ever gets a new trial
    and justice dances through
    and he is released
    you can bet they'll find another activist
    to agitate or worse
    the f.b.i. always excels in that.
in the place where finding enough room
    to collapse after being beat up
    with an empty constitution is exercise,
    uniforms are counted and
    instead of medicine bags
    there are tablets to swallow amnesia.

a picture of a brother's family ends up
    in a toilet bowl next to a collage
    of burning feathers
maybe you think it's the man
    with the broken thumb who dunnit.
he's laughing and using his tongue
    as a verb as he clicks his teeth
    like a revolver but even he cried
    at halloween and said
    it must be somebody's birthday.

I walked into a flower store selling
    purple dandelions and used 3-D glasses.
blew my mind.

people asked who's that on your t-shirt,
    george harrison right
    or is that tevye the fiddler?
i'm getting ready to jump in
    and tell them about peltier
    who sits above my heart
    with a safety pin scowl
    and such open eyes
    but the people just go thick into memory
    and tell me their favorite beatles song.
it's easier to talk about music
    than barbed wire meals.
it's simpler to talk about harmonicas
    and g chords than hear skeptics
    who generalize men,
    shout jack abbott was creative and
    got out, killed and came back
    like reciting nursery rhymes
    traveling underground sewers
    where even the water is afraid
    of being strangled by sand.

I whisper today eleanor rigby
    is my favorite song.

suddenly someone with green hair
    and loud pointy shoe footsteps
    (though in barefeet)
    says you know I know just how you feel.
I tried to wear a vote sid vicious pin
    on my mom's turtleneck sweater
    and like the fabric wouldn't hold the pin
    though it was such a sincere pin
    made in hong kong as it were

the sex pistols were big real gigantic there
and well anyway I tried to pin it
to my hair and that didn't work either
so I just bought a cappucino and left
a note for the busboy at club pajamas
to meet me left of the crayon toupees
near the alphabet soup and he was there
by now I wore the pin on my bra
and he screamed and rushed off to listen
to an all guitar band do tuba solos.
she gave me her business card.
it said socially conscious parfumerie and musk.
she smiled and gleefully confided
      with a matter of fact tone,
"i'm wearing riot — we're having trouble
      keeping civil disobedience
      and free peace in stock."
recycled bottles, non-violent and non-toxic.
I thought we'd all probably end up smelling
      like joan baez
      and the spirit of abbie hoffman.

it was a lot easier when I painted goldfish
      on my cheekbones and read *moby dick*
      to the dock workers.
I called it environmental literature.
it used to go over well at seaworld
      but gasoline costs too much
      to get to san diego regularly.

leonard peltier is the silence
      between every heartbeat
      and the beat itself blurring.
he gets little pieces of window taken away
      from him each month.

he's world war three.
little big world war one started
    with christopher columbus.
tiny big world war two was little big horn.
small big world war three is wounded knee.
    1890 to the present.
it's all the passions shot at
    in continuous battles.

I found a letter written by ghosts
    with a thousand questions and spins.
babies who knew a toll free number
    for amnesty international
    before they could walk.
I read verbatim.
daddy, we remember the world
    you want to change.
momma, we remember the world we entered.
our diapers were bullet holes.
our highchair was missing in action.
our dolls were lost with the healing bags.
our souls live for always up in the sun.
the love sparkles in the air
    and the green of the natural world.
daddy, we are not angry with you.
we are innocent of guilt and we go on.
we are the past, present
    and the days to come.
our tongues make music.
our lips tell stories.
momma, our breasts still need milk and
    human kindness where you gave plenty.
you sought the native american dream.

peace and harmony with minerals and people
    and beautiful names for children
and arson looks different than campfires
    where we prayed for tolerance and rain.
we know you loved us and will always love us.
mommy and grandma feed us corn
    and buffalo every day.
we will never go hungry.
daddy, eat well.
daddy, please let the great spirit
    dry your eyes.
let the four winds let you sleep
    in comfort tonight.

the letter crumbled into a cave
    meant for such wisdom.

the heart is a t-shirt saying
    read me
    understand what I need
    and care about my cares
we hide behind worldly posture
    in a world together.

we must never forget the strength in chanting.
breakfast chants.
love chants.
arlo guthrie chants.
so does woody guthrie and woody allen.
and elvis presley
    but not in the vegas years as much.
the grateful dead chant in their sleep.
allen ginsberg chants
    in someone else's sleep.
bob dylan chants that's a given.

this land was chanted
    before the ancestors stole it.
now nobody claims
    it's an enchanting place to live.
that is an irony lost
    on all the corporate fiends
    muzzled in ledgers
    and attache case combination locks.
children and women become warriors
    when the right to chant is taken away.

now the earrings of the trail of tears
    are wet in my hand.
the story was in motion.
the frybread was delicious.
one anthropologist's "artifact"
    is another man's food.
the jukebox was draped with a robbie conal
    "it can't happen here"
poster of george bush.

george bush is the 41st president in a row
    to break treaties.
america god shed his blame on thee
    for needing earrings that
    the war builders will say
    look so nice with that dress honey
    and will refuse to see the flood as
    anything but another accessory to pinch at.

UMBILICAL CORD

I feel like your umbilical cord
    must be dancing in a seashell
    somewhere off the
    island of lake michigan
    where the coast is clear
    except for memory and icebergs
    and dinosaurs
    who love to walk on water.

you go back to an old time
ancient is the tongue
    that sips lemonade and encyclopedia
    copper and snake
    within the radius
    of architecture and sea.

you know the difference
    between hero and sandwich
    between orchards and carmen miranda
    between tonsils and gramophone
    between spark and scarecrow.

you know where
    the world's tallest thermometer is
    and where it isn't.

you know where
    the singing telegram
    got a lump in its throat.

you know where
    the slot machines are
    that screech with all levers
    in a permanent outstretched volume

humans are as dispensable
    as oranges and cherries
    in a las vegas of the mindset.

you know the keys to the cities
    are in the bookstores and the trees.

you know most people
    threw away their vocal chords
    along with their butterflies
    the first time the net was dangled
    in their cereal and it looked
    like a mirage above the t.v. trays.

all the dreams of the world
    get chased around
    like dogs circling their tales
    like wedding trains
    dragging the stomp of idea
    the clang of blues
    and the registry
    of the store of open eyes.

somewhere in the place
    where goggles protect
    the pupil from chlorine,
    where the vision is spared
    the splinters from flying interference

    there should be an eyelid
    as big as a heartbeat,
    with your wink
    and your refusal to sleep.

ALL THIS 'CAUSE YOU'VE DOUBTED
THAT YOU HAVE YOUR OWN

I wanted under your wing
    where I could be wild
    where I could be water in a storm

I wanted under your wing
    where I could learn to swim
    learn to eat
    learn to trust

I wanted under your wing
    where animals hide
    to change to light
    where people go to breathe
    when they need oxygen

I wanted under your wing
    where music burned my ear
    where apples tasted like sugar
    or was it the other way around?

I wanted under your wing
    but you thought I meant under your cock.
I wouldn't kiss you there
I was horny for the wet spot on your wings
    knowing you had flown before
    and this time I wanted to come along.

But you took scissors
    and clipped your wings
    as I stared wide-eyed
    then nobody could fly

By denying me you sacrificed yourself.
We hid from each other
    until I realized
    you didn't really have wings
    you had shadows to constrict me

You had fish you had stolen
    from the innocence of the sea
You had seen to it that I'd grow
    turtle shells on my breasts,
    I'd grow coral reefs in my heart
Seaweed handed me a bouquet.
Solitude becomes a burden
    when you do not choose it.

Wings are temporary.
They are a big responsibility.
They itch.
They fall in the toilet when you sit down.
They get in the soup
    when you try to cook dinner.

People gave up wings awfully quick.
Some went heavy into some other direction.

You took out your penis
    and started flapping
You said suck on this
    let this pacify you

I said that doesn't look like a wing to me.

He said I've captured angels and witches
    I'm paranoid of everyone now
    do you want to what or what?

I said angels take the time
    to meet the spirit in your muscles.
He said I don't have the time
    and I said sounds like you do.

I hear a clock in your voice
    pleading for more.
needing something you almost have.
feel the dreams
    about to sweat off your body.
feel the hand
    reaching out to the piano.

Wings fell on me like hats.
Wings fell on my fingers like gloves
    but I didn't have less freedom.

Is this being my own hero?

With one look he said
    I will punish you for your stubbornness
    woman, I'll show you by wearing you down
    I'll make your sleep full of rocks
    and bridges with biting balloons
    that you'll be too traumatized to enter.
you'll go nowhere.

I said
    all this 'cause
    I can't find your wings.

He said no
    all this 'cause you've doubted
    that you have your own.

I HAVE FALLEN 3 TIMES

I have fallen 3 times.
    once while Barry Manilow sang
    It's Just Another New Year's Eve.
    once on a welcome mat.
    once while sweeping.

I am in physical therapy for the last fall.
Just recently I stopped the crutches
    and the knee immobilizer.
I noticed people were nicer to me
    when I was on crutches.
    nicer than usual.
I mean strangers.
Being a bit of a wild-haired, hippie-looking
    pin-wearing, hat-headed woman,
    I tend to stick out.
Total strangers asked me how I was doing
    with the crutches under my arms.
Young hip kids didn't stick
    their tongues out at me.
It seemed people could relate to an injury
    even if they couldn't relate to my
    Free Peltier pin.
People could relate to a hobbling hippie
    better than a room full of anarchists
    and purple wallpaper.

I wonder how it would have been
    if I had been in a wheelchair.

People can see themselves
    easily on crutches.
Not as commonly can they see themselves
    unable to stand up.
People are frightened
    by what they can't see
    as ever happening to them.
Fear turns to hatred almost simultaneously.
People hate seeing what exists
    and is possible.
People do many things
    to cover up their vision,
    refusing to see.

During a recent war
    people whispered right in front of me
    about my pins.
The pins were not specifically
    about a particular war,
    they were political pins I wear
    all the time.

I don't know how well the people
    could read the pins.
They stood in their corner
    clucking their prejudice at me,
    their right wing stained with blood,
    talking about the merits of body bags.
They saw me as a threat
    to their comfort zone.
I was a symbol of a circus.
I was rope burns of a trapeze artist.

What if everyone actually is
     a one person pied piper?
They didn't like the taste of the air
     after my song.
During the war I felt people
     almost decide to punch me.
I brought out extremes in people.
This was a day a hermit cried
     on my shoulder and said
     didn't Nietzsche say
     whatever doesn't kill you
     makes you stronger?

He was playing frisbee with his dog
     but instead of frisbees
     they threw records.
The dog caught *Highway 61 Revisited*
The man caught *Deja Vu*
I saw a stack of Joni Mitchell records
some Leonard Cohen
some Jack Kerouac

He said it's good karma
     to fill the air with music
Music not missiles is my motto
     think it'll catch?
I said it makes more sense than crystals.

He said the war gets to me.
I used a record needle to shoot up.
Now I realize I was just trying
     to breathe chords of joy again.
I thought injecting songs
     would make me happy.

All I had to do was be aware of the music
        and I became music.
Pretty trippy, huh?

He said outrun the liars
        they are so bent on mind control
        they are banning *War And Peace*
        they claim there never was a war.

I spent a day plastering fliers
        and shouting through a megaphone,
        "Don't feed the Pentagon!"
        when people treat each other
        without compassion
        we are adding to the military build-up.

There are no shortages of wars.
The war against the fat woman
        is a war that's been waged
        by a diverse army,
        from the idiot to the
        should have known better.
I say the war against the fat woman
        because this society
        has different agendas
        for different genders.

The fat man has a beer belly
        which shows he has the luxury
        to sit in front of the TV
        watching football games.
Acceptable American behavior.

The fat woman has no self control.
How can she expect to catch a man
        looking like that?
How could she let herself go that way?
Many times I have been teased for my looks
        or my weight or anything
        and everything by men
        void of conventionality themselves.
They were looking for an easy scapegoat.
They needed to seem taller
        by stepping on someone.

Whether we like it or not
        psychology spins insight
        in a collision course
        with our minds
and sure I understand
        the doctor, the corporation,
        and the government are in cahoots
        as they hand me a weight chart
        and say "Ellyn you are ruining
        the economy and the landscape
        cause you refuse to be like everybody else."

What percentage of fat
        is destructive to health?
What percentage of teasing and hating
        is destructive to health?
Just what is normal?

I once read a book so great
    everyone should read it
Shadow on a Tightrope edited by
    Lisa Schoenfielder and Barb Weiser.
It's how fat separates humans.
It's how fat brings people together.
It's in finally seeing with your heart.

I once read a book so fantastic
    called *In The Spirit of Crazy Horse*
    by Peter Matthiessen.
It's how race separates humans.
It's how race brings people together.
It's in finally seeing with your heart.

I once read a book called
    Nice Jewish Girls edited by
    Evelyn Torton Beck.
It's how sexual preference separates humans.
It's how sexual preference brings people together.
It's in finally seeing with your heart.

hey I'll spare you:
I've read a lot of books.

I hope people realize
    painful as my falls have been
they don't come close
    to the falls I've experienced
    when being knocked down by others.

YOM KIPPUR BLUES

In a few days it is heavy holy stuff
    going down in synagogues
    around the world.
It is organized religion.
It starts in the evening.
I can dig the service
    but I have been put under pressure
    to attend the whole service
    and nothing but the service 'cause
    my dad would be buying the tickets.

I can go for the singing.
I can go for the praying.
I can go for the shaloms
    but I can't go
    for the having to be there
    the entire time
    if I don't feel like it.
Spontaneously I might decide
    to listen to Beethoven,
Or I might need to see someone
    who almost was my lover.
Or I might decide to eat
    lentil soup in a restaurant
    that also has a bowling alley.
Someone might need me to listen.
Someone might need me to talk.
I might want to dance to Arlo Guthrie's hair.
I might learn harmonica.
I might fall out of love.
I might fall in love.
Maybe I'll read the liner notes
    of *Bringing It All Back Home.*

Perhaps I'll start wearing my soul
    like Joan Baez.
I could daydream about underground newspapers
    I publish in my heart,
      full of funnies, full of giddiness
      full of obituaries.
I would like to throw salt
    over my shoulders.
I would like good hands
    on my shoulders.
I would like to spend the night
    with the moon.
I would like to walk into the synagogue
    for one second and feel all the Kaddish
    and Bibles do a can-can dance
    and hear rabbis with eyes
    that take in Kabbalah prophets
    and can recite the songs
    on *Highway 61 Revisited.*
I want holiness.
I want revelation.
I want Leonard Cohen and Jerry Garcia
    to wake up fighting over me.
I don't want temples to charge $185
    for a seat and a yarmulke,
I can play a Warren Zevon record
    and get the same thing, dig.
I don't want Yiddish to be a lost language.
I speak it with my jaw.

There is wisdom in the humidity of ceilings.
There are weddings that take place
    only in my piece of wedding cake.

There are Bas Mitzvahs
    that make children adults.
There are Bas Mitzvahs
    that make adults children.
I get suspicious
    when I hear a person is a good Christian.
I get suspicious
    when I hear I am a Christkiller.

I get Hebrew schools forming on my profile,
    my hair, my mystic circumstances.
I might marry someone
    from another background.
I want my family to know
    that it was love and bless us.
I don't want guilt like some Tower of Babel
    strangling my larynx.
The ceremonies of cantors
    live in my pillowcase.
I rock back and forth in my laughter.
I look both ways before I eat shellfish.
I keep Kosher in my soul.
I live for love.
The serenity prayer rests
    on the roof of my mouth.
The intensity prayer paints my lips
    with hunger and beads.
My dad says remember you're Jewish.
As though I have amnesia or something.
As though I wasn't knocked
    happily unconscious once
        by the point of a Jewish star.

I wear purple tights
    and leg warmers to temple.
The Fairfax men smile.
I find the Torah is a plate
    my dreams eat off.
I just don't want to be told 30 hours
    in synagogue is automatically better
    than 30 seconds.
Marc Chagall stained glass windows
Fiddler on the Roof soundtrack
Shoah on public television

Like the Indians who believe
    in no separation of religion and life
I too pray in the air
    regardless if it is
    Temple Stephen Wise or McCabe's
    'cause Loudon Wainwright III is there.
The address of holiness is the
    mystic wobbling when I am
    passionate about someone or something.
My dad is probably going to say
    that damn hippie daughter of mine is
    losing touch with her ancestors.
I say no.
I have never felt more a part
    of my family tree.
I stand up on the branch
I admire the shade.
I build tree houses (everyone can come in)
    even though I can't boil noodles that well.
I stare at a picture of Bob Dylan.
I read a page of Allen Ginsberg.

I conduct Rosh Hashanah
There are no collection plates.
There are no dues.
There are no fancy clothes
  and like the traditional rabbis
  on holy days I wear tennis shoes.
I could be a hermit
  except the warmth eats my shadow.
I could be a socialist.
I could be a cafeteria leftist
  who only has liver and sour cream.
I could be the first college dropout
  to major in the eternal singalong
  of John Prine's *Angel from Montgomery*.

I hum.
(The congregation rises)
I get nookie from Isaac Bashevis Singer.
What could be more Jewish than that?

AN OPEN LETTER TO JOSEPH CAMPBELL

a grateful deadhead delivers my mail, man
yeah like I live in a garden
    and in a calendar that zigzags seasons
    and I get lots of personal junk mail
    and a deadhead gives it to me
he looks like jerry, man, jerry garcia
well, how jerry looked 15 years ago
god we all got older after 'nam
    kent state, watergate
so it's like I rent this purple walled maze
    and I kick down the walls and wow
    I got space, for my bootlegs, man
    and for my candles and incense
    when I get in the mood
    you know what I say
yeah and this guy with a couple hundred pins
    saying up with this
    down with that
    25¢ newspapers
    lies sponsored by the government
    and he had sideburns shaped like
    50's automobiles along his left cheek
    a guitar on the other
he held a transistor radio playing
    walk me out in the morning dew
    and when that finished
    he would yodel *lather*
    by jefferson airplane
man it was good so good
those were 27 hour days
well me I was poor
    so nobody was writing me no letters

it was a couple of years too late
    for poor to be hip
like free provos bicycle rides
    through amsterdam was through man
richard brautigan was still dancing
    books though
those were some days
man I wore black and purple
(cause I know he dug my vibes)
    when I heard brautigan blew himself off
I know where I was
    in a hungarian midnight mass
    madhatter island

I'm jewish but I was there cause I went with
    my almost lover eric's dad's girlfriend
    yeah
eric was in london buying trousers
    with mirrors and camus novels
eric proofread textbooks for a living
I grew pumpkins in central park
well like anyway I used to get bills
I called them government vampire-grams
    cause they like wanted me to pay taxation
    and there was a hell of a lot of misrepresentation
    and like money for light
    shit, what happened to the sun
    what's, you know, wrong with natural, man
I sent washington some free granola petitions
I spent 3 months in jail
didn't have the bread to get free myself
    but I was sort of free
    you know, in my way
    as dylan says, watch your parking meters

in prison I started smoking cigarettes
they beat my hands
        and it hurt too much to read books
damn them, you know, they hadn't like
        invented those thingamajiggies
        that turn pages by windmill
there are a lot of people, up people
        who wanted to read in the poke
        but there were attacks on our fingers
        like stopping our flow of knowledge
        spirit stompers
        they did what they could to reduce
        the men to hard-ons
        and the women to playboy crucifixes
my dump cost a pile of cum now
then I was happy to have like beads going
        from one room to another
it was cool till I saw marlo thomas
        on *that girl* had the same apartment
t.v. only was good when it was off
I knew how to turn it off

remember when dostoevsky was sold
        in the russian subways
yeah man I like to read
now the most literate people listen
        to cassettes of books in their car o.k.
I think people enjoy feeling words
I like haven't taken a survey
        but I bet the blind prefer braille
        to tapes cause it's more there
so I used to get polyester velvet
        invitations to happenings

now I get a free espresso maker
    if I consider buying a new car
if it rains my mailman says it's beautiful
    god loves the garden
if it snows he says groovy
    mother nature coughing ice cream
if it's sunny he just grins and plucks his cheek
    and sings along with jerry
    you know, jerry garcia
my mailman is named turquoise glitter
    (on my library card, he laughs) he digs
    joplin, gracie and pigpen
    reads comic books with subtitles
    (just like opera) and he only
    delivers underground newspapers
    fuck the los angeles times, he says
    crumple the lies
glitter told me the worst trip he ever had
    was eating frozen yogurt
    in westwood nation while bon jovi
    played knx-fm
glitter told me he feels old sometimes
one day, he said, the world will end
    when deadhead vans won't be allowed
    overnight parking at arenas
he hyperventilated and wiped his sideburns
man, he said it again, man
last tuesday I found out glitter was asked
    to deliver mail in century city
it seemed sad, you know, like singing
    along for three minutes
    of *puff the magic dragon*
    only to be like really bummed out

I have a generic mailperson now
I get the bills at the same time
        every afternoon
I asked hey what type of music do you like?
the mailman said, "oh me? all kinds"
I nodded and waited for some, like, details
I got silence
        and the repeated phrase, all kinds
oh shit, glitter baby, you always mumbled
        freedom of choice
        is wasted on the indecisive

yesterday I found a neon boot in my mailbox
        and a note from glitter
        it said gone to taos to study the wind
        want to, like come?
I packed
I tossed my hair like marlo thomas
        and I took a book on
        the spiritualism of centipedes
        unlike marlo thomas
        and packed for 40 days and 40 nights
        at the least, man

MY MIND IS A RADIO

my mind is a radio
once I could sing
    the play by play of *Blonde on Blonde*
    like it was Eddie Doucette weaving
    basketball free throw averages
    with a handful of scars

every day I listened to all Dylan
    all of the times they are a changin'

I sat in a rockin' roll chair
my own Edward Hopper painting

my eyelids showing outtakes
    from *Renaldo and Clara*
    and *Eat The Document*
    to the amphitheater
    between retina and lash

in the constant narration of survival
    so many concerts take place
    in rooms wearing the glow
    of loneliness like a shadow
    wallpaper hovering
    as the edges
    lift around us
    like the struggle
    between the octopus
    and the straightjacket

society pushes the flailing
        into the arms of a tarantula
        quicker than one can pronounce *conscience*
ostrich eating has taken on the mythology
        of folklore and knives

        proving for once and for all
        you are what you eat

there is a price
        for sitting in your underwear
        as your bathrobe opens and closes
        like an accordion

the price of solitude is going up

there is a price
        for knowing who James Baldwin is

there is a cost to keeping a calendar
        on your desk that goes beyond 1492

there is a price for uttering
        what's on the tip
        of most peoples' tongues
        like an ulcer

if chewing an apple a day
        keeps the doctor away
what does sharing culinary
        recipes and utensils
        with the serpent
        do for the measuring cup

we are measured in doses
    of how much we can take
    and not play dead
the sky is bruised as one billion
    are served the illusion
    throwing their arms up in the air
    simultaneously goose shrugging
I am not really an amnesiac
I only play one in America

they recite their pledge
    to the Tower of Babel
    and Babylon's suburbs
    in perfect pitch

9 to 5 work
6 to 12 t.v.
1 to 8 sleep
wow! am I happy!

ticket master holds no stubs
    for concerts I've held in my ear drum
benefits for my endorphins

culling multi-media
kaleidoscopic, arthroscopic

horoscope-specific
spectacles
just for me

laser light shows for the nearsighted
costumes from the summer stock production
    of *Hair*
    make-up by Tupperware
in many living rooms
    the breathing wait
    for oxygen and a welcome mat
reassurance, an eleven letter word

every word can be turned
    into an infinite letter word

talking blues
the holiest newspaper
    leaves its topicality
    and timelessness around
    the world's mouth
    like a saxophone reed

a curling iron turns our hair into waves
a cattle iron turns people into fetal balls
    afraid to make waves

there are concerts that make the largest parade
    seem to move with the fragility
    and vitamin of haiku

music has its vocabulary
    as thrilling as any balmy thesaurus,
    it can be a demonstration
    with its own ebbs and flows

monotones fill the sky
    with lockjawed stars

the clock strikes war
        from the moment one wakes
        to the moment one falls down

we live in the space
        between Salvador Dali's moustache
        and his paintbrush whiskers
        and keep time to his teeth
        and we get imaginary punches
        in the imagination for punishment

and the floor is stained with everything
        from metaphysics to blood

music comes like an ambulance
        like a ladybug
music comes with binoculars
        and a telescope
music comes with astronomy

when a house of cards falls
        a person crawls into the netherworld
        of diamonds and clubs

hearts scatter like ice cubes disappeared
        in hell's hot air

when a house of sheet music topples
        Maria Callas
        and Joan of Arc
        giggle like girls

THE COWARDICE OF AMNESIA

10 9 8 7 6 5 4 3 2 1
tulips full of smog
    sense pollution
    mouth full of hunger
    cost of living skyscrapers
    ozone laryngitis
    torn & bloody trees
    swastikas coming in the middle of
    the night to landscape

the stitch-stitch of commerce and
    needlepoint flags with 50 (or is it 51 bloody stars?)
    that keep fainting into fists
express lanes for National Enquirer
asbestos in sack lunches
scheduled arsons
General Custer returning in other masks
Bibles full of evangelist semen
    and midwestern 700 Club housewife
    bowling for religion dollars
my breath leans into a billboard
crowded industrial districts with sofas
    and TV and windchimes in the closet
    making it seem like a home atmosphere
complicated telephone booths where superman
    loses our clothes and our wishbones are
    broken with one deliberate massage
whom can you trust?
the newspaper ink runs off into lies
    in your hand,
    aren't you paranoid?
    don't trust the encyclopedias

historians have been bribed
on chocolate mornings
and nobody respects 'em in the night

answering machines of the presidential face
that shoots poison
out of the flower store chain
he opened in Bitburg
head scratchers in the psychological bubble
forgetting
50 minute clock watchers
putting the sun on a pulley
because so much chemical spit has tired her
whiplash the moon
when you shut your eyes don'tcha see
the storyboards on your eyelids
and don't try to cry
the nuclear power profit king named Scar
comes with straws and princes
and in the idle moments when your back
was turned, put your tears in boxes
you need to keep your distance from
and touch only with rusted fingertips
that you seem to lose anyway.

the gauze takers in the hospitals read
Fahrenheit 451 as the pages
go up in blue smoke,
desperate needles shaped like nickels
go in search of someone with a drop
of water to steam the bandages
of the ill and the cynics who were
tortured by the grinning police who beat
and punch the elbows of people who aren't
smiling.

still looking for water
    the oceans turned to mud.
Loch Ness is found on Skid Row.
fish walking into mass graves.
mermaids reading Kafka.
the anthropologist/doctors wearing
    stethoscopes that look strangely
    like keno cards find a man
    who has been on the cover
    of *People/Person/More People/People Blah/*
    People the Shopping Mall as Icon/
    (the bookstores don't sell anything
    but magazines & unauthorized biographies)

Mr. 1984 1/2 Epic Syntaxguy the 3rd
    has had a life of ease and status.
triple car garages in his bathroom.
he has poodles stand in movie lines for him
    then he asks the dogs
    who directed the film?

Epic has pin-up posters of microwave ovens
    in his house.
he worships technology
    and no apologies are ever given.
the strawtakers fear him
    and the census shadows show he's 96
    and in good health.
the camera pans across his shirt
    that says *what, me, care?*
suddenly he screams out *hi mom!*
his mother is 17 (Epic's dad liked girls
    who were too young to vote)

a tear fell from his right eye.
there was pandemonium.
that was the first tear in eighteen months
     anyone had seen.
Bob Hope walked into the room
     and gave him a medal
     and a charge card for diesel.
seeing Bob Hope made Epic satisfied
     and he died instantly.

nobody tried to start his heart.
they went for his eyes
     but of course the water had dried up
     in cartoon images of meeting
     his wonderful Bob
     played over and over in his mind.

lo and behold the people fell silent.
all at once an idea lifted the drooping humans.
they would go at midnight into graves
     and steal water from any eyes
     filled with tears,
it was called the theory of Robin Hood
     or Oedipus
     whichever you prefer,
there were bound to be a few ounces
     of clear clean water in those dead eyes.

tearing up graves was fun the people said.
look at all the gold.
look at all the silver.
they forgot about the water.

WHO'S GONNA TALK ABOUT
THE SUNFLOWERS NOW

it seems marrow is running through the sand glass
    as time asks
    who will remember Blake
    who will not forget the chords of ghosts.

there is a vase full of fingerprints
    and sawdust
    with a memory of whistling
    and horses pulling sugar cubes
    from a salt mine.

there is somebody who dresses up
    a sunflower like a scarecrow,
    saying I saw faces in those buds
    and it frightened me.

there is a merry-go-round called world
    making dizzy and what comes down
    must stay down predictions
    on the coins that sit on eyes
    defying light to enter this copper
    this metal.

and someone pulls the petals off the flowers
    with a greed and a jaded penmanship.

someone talks in botany to someone who
    listens in a flood
    to the irony of umbrellas.

someone walks through the world
    calling a parasol a parasol.

the molecules keep changing.
Allen Ginsberg answered *present* at the school yard
    swinging the liberty bell
    between his teeth.

Death shakes all the particles up like a
    snow crusted souvenir
    of a sled, a dog and a river

but when the dog wags his tail
    and the river becomes an amusement park
there is a sigh of relief
    as though the log ride
    is anything more than a metaphor
    for most trips carrying
    a mirror down memory lane.

People are sneezing
    and the flowers are taking it hard.

War is unkind to pollen
    and other living things.

There is somebody right now smelling
    the irises of Van Gogh
    in the backyard of a trauma
    that's running THX through the swim
    of their nasal passage

Somebody is going into a store
    asking for bulbs with their fragrance
    their name and a monogrammed shovel.

Somebody is asking how many bulbs does it take
    to screw in a flower.

The answer is always people.